Special thanks to all of the people at Conway Management who helped in the writing, design and production of this book.

Conway Management Company, Inc.
15 Trafalgar Square
Nashua, New Hampshire, 03063 USA
603-889-1130 • 800-359-0099 • Fax: 603-889-0033
www.conwaymgmt.com

D0949371

10   9

To: The Users of Waste Chasers[©]

The Right Way To Manage[©] is a management system that results in improved organizational performance through the continuous improvement of work and work processes. It enables organizations to please external customers with products and services those customers want, when and where they want them, at prices they are willing to pay. Success with this system requires four important elements:

Will—urgent desire, resolution, determination

Belief—conviction: true belief comes only from doing—that is, being directly involved in the action for improvement

Wherewithal—required resources
- Capital (money), technology and equipment
- The tools—human relations, simple and sophisticated statistics, industrial engineering (the plan, study, change and improvement of work), imagineering, waste identification and elimination, customer-supplier relationship and surveys

Doing—action for improvement, change. The actual doing is the easiest part. The hard part is getting everyone aligned toward common goals forever

Continuous improvement is the key to success in any organization. At Conway Management Company we know the key to improvement is finding, quantifying and eliminating waste through continuous process improvement. *Waste Chasers*[©]

contains the tools to make continuous improvement a reality.

Now, in one small book, you have the tools that you need. Everyone in your organization should have these tools in his or her pocket ready for immediate use.

Sincerely,

Bill Conway

William E. Conway
Chairman & Chief Executive Officer

Preface

This pocket guide is based on the system of management developed by William E. Conway. The System has its roots in the principles of Dr. W. Edwards Deming. This book can be used alone as a guide to continuous business improvement in quality and productivity, or as a supplement to Mr. Conway's book *The Quality Secret: The Right Way To Manage*[©].

The Quality Secret is that the elimination of the waste in a process automatically improves the quality coming from that process. By reducing the problems and variation in a process, stabilizing it, and producing what the customer wants, you can achieve high, consistent quality at low cost.

The Right Way To Manage[©] is a system and a methodology to achieve high quality and low cost by eliminating waste in all the work and work processes. For more than 20 years, Bill Conway and the people at Conway Management have developed the principles of continuous improvement into a detailed, practical management system used by leading companies throughout the world.

WASTE is the difference between the way things are now and the way things could be if everything were right—no errors, troubles, problems or complexities.

The Way Things Could or Should Be

The Waste

The Way Things Are Now

Waste can be as large as 20-50% of a company's sales or an organization's funding or budget, and is a major reason for lack of competitiveness. The concepts, tools and techniques described in this guide are critical to:

- Finding the waste
- Getting rid of it
- Preventing its return—forever!

The tools described here are the fundamental language of continuous improvement. They are used to gather facts and data about the market, customers, work and work processes, and then turn them into useful information. Over time, everyone in an organization can and should learn to use them on a daily basis so that they become second nature.

The search for waste is ongoing. Since most of the waste is embedded in the work, we need to look at the work differently and more closely than we have before.

Waste comes in four major forms. Organizations waste material, capital, time, and the opportunities that could lead to increased sales and/or profit. Traditionally, organizations concentrate on the waste of materials and capital. Actually, the biggest waste of all is the lost sales or opportunities that we could have had if everything were right. One of the largest contributing factors to this waste is the ineffective use of people's time, energy and brain power. This is a result of the management systems and processes, not the people. Huge gains can be made by focusing on improving processes, rather than blaming people. The tools and principles necessary to support the attack on waste are shown in **The Model**.

The Model

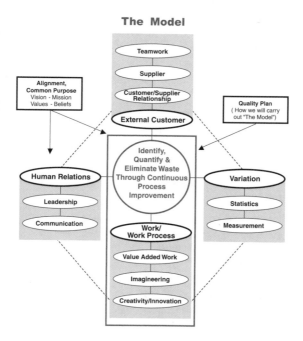

Table of Contents

Why & How To Use This Book

This handbook provides a convenient reminder of the tools and principles required for continuous improvement. It is designed to help solve both the technical and human problems encountered on the path to running an effective organization that creates and delivers value, providing high quality and low cost products and services that meet or exceed customer needs and wants.

Quality is process driven. To improve the quality of a product or service, you must improve the process(es) that produce and support that product or service. Quality alone is not enough. It must be achieved in a way that minimizes costs and maximizes productivity.

This achievement requires a continuous effort to **identify, quantify and eliminate waste in all of the work and work processes**. Eliminating the waste improves the quality of the work process which in turn improves the quality and consistency of the product or service produced. **Rooting out the waste and preventing its return is the core activity of The Right Way To Manage©.** This approach works for all processes, not just manufacturing. It can be used to eliminate waste in the processes of marketing, selling, research and development, administration, finance, etc. It has been used for all of the processes and systems in oil and gas exploration, government service, supermarkets and more. It can also be applied to your personal life.

This handbook is divided into three sections. The

first describes the basic tools of variation, which include the simple charting techniques. These tools convert data into useful information. They help organize the information in a way that allows you to see the waste and measure your progress in eliminating it. These tools help people communicate a problem and focus on <u>facts</u>, rather than opinions about the <u>work</u>, rather than the people.

The second section covers work and work processes. All waste comes from what you work on and how you do the work. This section will help you discover what work you do that adds value from the customers' viewpoint. It begins with a detailed description of how to analyze the work being done and how to identify those parts of the work which add value. This section also covers techniques used to eliminate unnecessary work and to do the remaining work more effectively.

The final section focuses on implementing change. It outlines the elements needed to achieve the desired change. It suggests how to tap the brain power of all the people involved in a process – suppliers, operators and customers – to achieve continuous improvement.

The process improvement methodology outlined on page 19 describes a proven series of steps to guide you through systematically improving a process. It suggests tools and concepts contained in this book that can be used at each step. Use this guide, along with the table of contents, to find the tools you need. The following chart is also helpful.

Identifying, Quantifying & Eliminating Waste

If You	You Need	Then Do
Are curious...	Ideas...	Brainstorm areas of waste
Know where the waste is	Priorities	Quantify the waste; use Pareto chart
Have decided what to work on	Project definition	Develop team charter, select project team, develop project plan
Have a defined project	Starting point	Learn about the processes, e.g., - draw process flow chart - gather process data Fix obvious problems
Understand the process	Reasons for problems	Analyze flow charts Draw fishbone charts Analyze process data with run/control charts & histograms Imagineer what the process could or should look like
Know reasons for problems	Possible solution	Brainstorm possibilities
Have possible solutions	How to proceed	Develop selection criteria. Pick preferred solution
Have a solution	Implementation	Develop an action plan to put the solution in place; carry out action plan
Have implemented the solution	Verification	Measure outcomes to see if the problem was solved. If not, go back to *Know reasons for problems*
Verified that the solution worked	Standardization	Permanently change the process. Document new process. Train people using the process. Keep measuring to ensure that the gains are kept. Look for other places to apply the improvements
Have locked in the gains	Decision on future steps	Decide whether further action is needed. Evaluate the team's effectiveness and share the learnings. Recognize and celebrate accomplishments

Concepts & Principles

The core activity of **The Right Way To Manage©** is to *continuously improve all work processes by identifying, quantifying, and eliminating waste.* This system looks everywhere for waste and reviews each activity and process to evaluate whether it adds value from the external customer's viewpoint and if it is performed in the most efficient and effective way.

The four forms of waste are waste of material, waste of capital, waste of time, and waste from lost sales or missed opportunities.

Work

- *All of the waste ultimately comes from work and the processes used to accomplish work.* In other words, waste results from what organizations work on and how they work. All forms of work can produce waste—work done by machines, chemical processes, computers and energy, as well as that done by people.

- *At least 50% of continuous improvement is working on the right things.* Constantly use the Pareto mentality (see Pareto Principle pg 35) to ensure that you are making the best decisions about what to work on.

- Eliminating waste requires a detailed knowledge of the work itself, the kind of knowledge that is held by the people operating the processes and the R&D people, engineers, supervisors, maintenance people, suppliers, etc. *Enlist the help of knowledgeable people to identify, quantify, and eliminate waste.*

- *If you truly eliminate the waste, the remaining work will be real value added work for your customer or work that is absolutely necessary to sustain the organization.* Strive constantly to improve the percentage of activities that add value while improving the way you do value added work.

- *Staff and schedule work so that employees have full time, value added work available at all times.* Work tends to expand to fill the available time. As you study and improve work, this will enable you to capture the gains and improve productivity.

- *Imagineering is a powerful tool for discovering waste. Imagineering is visualizing the way things would be if everything were perfect. By comparing current reality to perfection, you can see and quantify the "gap" or the waste.* Successful imagineering depends on gathering facts, truly understanding the purpose and customer requirements for a process, creatively questioning the work process, developing and systematically implementing a new process closer to perfection.

Customers & Suppliers

- *The underlying mission of any viable organization must be to please customers.* Pleasing customers requires communicating to understand their needs and wants. Successful organizations also anticipate what the customer will want in the future and make continuous improvements with those needs and wants in mind.

- ***The efficient production of quality goods and services for customers requires that suppliers also work in continuous improvement***. Successful organizations partner with their suppliers to develop the most effective and efficient ways to meet customers' requirements. Such partnerships require information sharing, excellent feedback systems and cooperation. Developing effective supplier partnerships enables organizations to minimize the number of suppliers they use while reducing the overall cost of doing business and improving the consistency of purchased inputs.

- ***The best possible marketing tool is to provide value to customers by furnishing high quality products or services that customers want at low cost***. This goal simplifies the overall marketing plan. High quality at low cost is also the path to real employment security.

Human Relations

- ***"Treat people as you would like to be treated"*** is the golden rule that encourages people to work in continuous improvement. Valuing people and their talents creates the environment in which continuous improvement thrives.

- ***The process or the system, not the individual, is responsible for 90% or more of all problems, waste, and missed opportunities***. Rather than blame individuals for problems, successful organizations enlist people's help to identify and eliminate those problems by studying, changing and improving work processes.

- *It should be in everyone's interest to share their knowledge of the best way to perform work.* Sharing and standardizing best practices is essential for delivering consistently high performance. Developing a culture that encourages sharing as well as adopting improved methods increases the amount and rate of organizational learning. It also fosters a team environment that enhances creativity, collaboration and excellence.

- *Work standards, numerical goals and objectives often artificially limit quality and productivity.* If people fear NOT meeting objectives, they tend to establish objectives they are sure they can readily meet. Develop effective ways to use goals and objectives to encourage risk-taking and continuous improvement.

- *Educate people so that they understand working on continuous improvement helps everyone and enables each person to help others.*

Variation

- *Variation exists in all things and all processes.* Reducing variation is the key to producing consistently high quality products or services. An understanding of the nature of variation is essential to taking appropriate action for improvement.

- ***The tools that identify, analyze, and communicate variation are key to finding and eliminating waste***. Charts of key process variables focus effort on the things that count, warn of adverse changes and enable you to measure progress.

- ***Control charts are invaluable in achieving, maintaining and improving a stable process***.

- ***Charts provide the means for measuring improvement***. Measuring progress helps to focus effort on the things that count and indicate when a new or different approach may be necessary.

Implementation

- ***To work as a cohesive team, people need the kind of common purpose provided by a mission statement that describes the basic function of the organization and a vision statement that describes the organization's ambitious, but realistic goals***. These statements are basic to providing the focus, direction, and constancy of purpose to keep everyone working together.

- ***"Vital Few" management directed projects should receive priority of resources and management attention.*** Management must identify those three to five projects most essential to achieving the vision in order to insure that critical things are accomplished and that efforts are not diluted. From these projects, many sub-projects will arise.

- **Leaders at every level must be leaders of change.** They take risks and set an example for continuous improvement by being active, visible participants in making changes.

- **Continuous improvement requires: a) the will to do it, b) the belief that it can be done, c) the wherewithal to accomplish it in the form of education and training, and d) action.** These four items make up the engine of continuous improvement. Leadership provides the energy to drive this engine and to make continuous improvement everyone's job, forever.

Process Improvement Methodology

The key to any process improvement, change or innovation is the use of the Plan-Do-Study-Act (PDSA) Cycle originally proposed by Walter Shewhart. Once waste, an opportunity or a project is identified, PDSA can and should be used for any process changes.

Plan: Identify the current situation; gather the data; imagineer (page 87) what the process could or should be like. Identify and analyze causes, identify root causes, and lay a plan for improvement

Do: Make the improvements, changes. Take action!

Study: Study the effect of changes, actions. Measure the results. Did the changes do what you expected or wanted? Is it okay, better, worse?

Act: If you are satisfied, standardize the improvements; plan for more improvements; if you are not satisfied, study the reasons why and plan for further actions.

Use the PDSA Cycle for small incremental process changes, to perform quick turnarounds within a work cycle, <u>and</u> for major system changes or process changes which may require more in-depth planning.

The following methodology describes a systematic way of implementing the PDSA cycle and lists the tools appropriate for each step. Page references are given for tools and techniques used in this methodology that are covered in *Waste Chasers*.

Conway Methodology

1. Search for opportunities; decide what to work on.

Identify the waste (pg 4 & Sec. 2)   Fishbone chart (pg 54)
4 Forms of waste (pg 5)   Flow chart (pg 44)
Surveys (pg 129)   Prioritization matrix (pg 94)
Pareto charts (pg 35)

2. Clearly define the project. Select the improvement team.

Problem statement *   Measurement (pg 105)
Team charter *   Brainstorm (pg 56)
Project plan *   Ground rules *

3. Study the current process/situation.

Check sheet (pg 27)   Histogram (pg 60)
Run chart (pg 30)   Pareto chart (pg 35)
Flow chart (pg 44)   Control chart (pg 75)
Fishbone chart (pg 54)   Affinity diagram (pg 90)
Imagineer (pg 87)

4. Analyze causes; plan the improvement.

Fishbone chart (pg 54)   Pareto chart (pg 35)
Imagineer (pg 87)   Brainstorm (pg 56)
Correlation chart (pg 70)   Histogram (pg 60)

5. Carry out the improvement plan.

Run chart (pg 30)   Flow chart (pg 44)
Histogram (pg 60)

6. Study the effect of the changes.

Run chart (pg 30)   Control chart (pg 75)
Histogram (pg 60)

7. Standardize the improved process.

Surveys (pg 129)   Run chart (pg 30)
Flow chart (pg 44)   Histogram (pg 60)

8. Assess progress and plan for the future.

Fishbone chart (pg 54)   Brainstorm (pg 56)
Pareto chart (pg 35)   Affinity diagram (pg 90)

* see Team Waste Chasers

Guidelines for Collecting Data

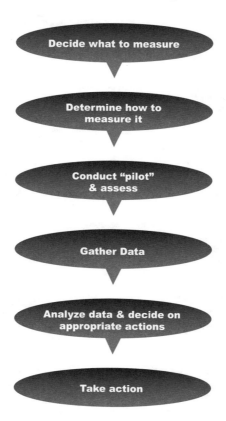

Decide what to measure

Determine how to measure it

Conduct "pilot" & assess

Gather Data

Analyze data & decide on appropriate actions

Take action

Tools to Get Information

Information You Want	Recommended Tools
Measures	- **Run chart or Control chart** - **Tally sheet** - **Histogram** Examples: - fill weight, density, pH, concentration - amount of downtime - line speed What to look for: - trends - shifts in the average - where the range of variation is centered
Counts	- **Check sheet** Examples: - type of error or complaint - number of off-spec units or rejects - products out-of-stock by type What to look for: - biggest opportunity for improvement
Process description	- **Process flow chart** Examples: - all the steps in the order entry process - time required for each step

Information You Want	Recommended Tools

What to look for:
- extra steps, delays, transport
- inspections
- other non-value added time
- redundancies

- Check list

Examples:
- list of steps in a procedure
- time required for each step

Ideas or opinions

- Brainstorming
- Fishbone chart (cause & effect diagram)

Examples:
- reasons for morale problems
- ways to improve customer service

What to look for:
- most important contributing factors

- Imagineering

Examples:
- description of a process "if everything were perfect"

What to look for:
- the gap between current reality and perfection

- Survey

<u>Examples</u>:
- customer survey to evaluate our
  performance
- employee survey

<u>What to look for</u>:
- biggest opportunities or most
  important

Section 1:

Tools of Variation

People in most organizations are flooded with data. Often, data in its raw form is difficult to use and analyze, so we employ some simple statistical tools to turn data into information. They can be used to discover the significance of data, and to make it easier to understand and communicate. Many of these tools are simple charts. Keep in mind that the purpose of gathering data and turning it into information is to provide a basis for action for improvement.

Check Sheet

A check sheet is a tool for recording occurrences of events. A check sheet uses check marks, x's or tick marks to show a count of items falling into various categories. It can take several different forms.

Making and Using a Check Sheet
When used to show how the output of a process varies, a process distribution check sheet provides a rough histogram of the data (page 64).

Check Sheet

Date: *9:30* **Product:** *MX Rods* **Machine:** *12*

Shift: *2nd*   **Prepared by:** *John Hobson*

14.1	14.2	14.3	14.4	14.5	14.6	14.7	14.8
			X				
		X	X				
		X	X				
		X	X	X			
	X	X	X	X			
	X	X	X	X			
	X	X	X	X	X		
	X	X	X	X	X	X	
	X	X	X	X	X	X	X
X	X	X	X	X	X	X	X
X	X	X	X	X	X	X	X

Diameter (mm.)

The check sheet does not reveal the sequence in which the data was taken. To highlight trends that occur over time, a run chart may be needed in addition to the check sheet.

When used to count defects, errors, issues or occurrences of various types, a check sheet can be a step in developing a Pareto chart (page 34).

Shipping Errors

Wrong Quantity	ЖЖ ЖЖ III
Wrong Product	ЖЖ II
Wrong Packaging	ЖЖ ЖЖ ЖЖ IIII
Wrong Address	ЖЖ III
Wrong Pricing	ЖЖ ЖЖ ЖЖ ЖЖ ЖЖ
Other	ЖЖ ЖЖ

A check sheet can also used to record the location of defects or activities by marking them on a drawing or floor plan. The pattern and location of the plotted points may provide clues as to the cause. For example, bubbles in a particular area of a plastic part may point to uneven pressure in forming as a cause. Or tick marks of errors on a blank invoice may point out which elements are most frequently wrong or missing.

? Questions to Ask

- What is the purpose of the check sheet? What are you trying to determine?
- Is the type of check sheet appropriate for the analysis you want? Is it simple to use? What charts will you want to turn it into? Pareto? Histogram?
- Do you need a run chart to show trends? If so, how can you collect the data in time sequence?
- Does the person collecting the data understand the importance of recording all the data? Does the person have a clear operational definition of the data to be collected? Will everyone who collects the data be able to do it in the same way with consistent results?
- Should the data be grouped? By location? By shift? By machine? By person? If so, can this be done with different colors or marks on the same check sheet? Or does it require separate check sheets?
- What will you do as a result of collecting data?
- What does the check sheet tell you about what action to take or what further information is needed?

! Points to Remember

- Ask the people who will collect the data for their input on the design and use of the check sheet.
- Make the check sheet user friendly.
- Field test the check sheet and make necessary adjustments to ensure accurate, reliable data.
- Decide what to do with the data.

Run Chart

A run chart is a line graph that plots the performance of a variable over a period of time. It allows you to see the level at which the process is operating as well as the amount of variation around the average. Use it to detect variation, trends and shifts in the average level of the process.

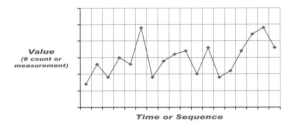

Making a Run Chart

Choosing the right things to measure is critical for any process. The measured element must be able to accurately reflect the performance of the process or variables in the process. Otherwise, the chart may be misleading. For example, only charting the *number* of defective pieces rather than the *percent* defective could reflect changes in production levels rather than changes in process effectiveness. Similarly, charting dollars of accounts receivable alone may not be as useful as charting dollars and the number of days' sales they represent. People pay attention to what is measured so choosing the right thing can affect behavior.

- The measured element should be a key performance variable, something that is critical to the process. Usually, these are measures of effectiveness (quality) or efficiency (time or cost). Effective measures include results measures, measures of key inputs and key process variables.

- Make data gathering as easy as possible. Ideally the people involved in the process should gather the data and update the charts.

- Update charts frequently. Seeing what happened in the last hour or day may be more valuable than seeing what happened last week or last month. When you start a chart, try to get some historical data. This will show you the operating level and variation in the current process.

- To design a run chart, draw a horizontal axis and mark it with the points of time when measurements will be recorded. On the vertical axis, mark the scale with the unit you are measuring (pounds, inches, % defective, errors, $, etc.). Construct the vertical scale in such a way that it covers the range you expect and accurately reflects the variation.

- Plot the data in order as it occurs over the time period selected.

- Draw a line showing the process average. This line may help reveal shifts and trends in the process. The average is often shown as $\bar{X}$.

- Use your understanding of variation to interpret the chart and decide on appropriate action.

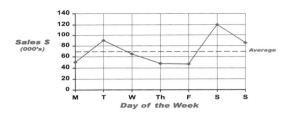

Using a Run Chart

The chart below shows a shift in the process average in the number of proposals completed per month.

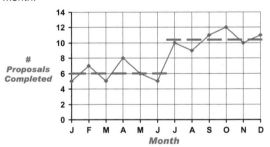

A new trend could also appear:

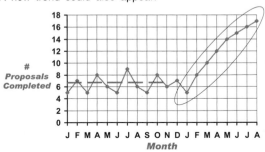

For more information on how to detect a trend, see control charts (pg 75)

Sometimes it is helpful to compare two similar processes by showing them on the same chart:

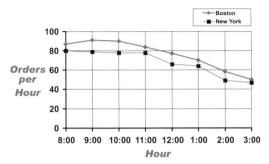

Besides the difference in production by office, the chart points out that production tends to drop later in each day.

A run chart gives visual clues about how a process is operating. It shows whether the process is improving, deteriorating, or staying the same. Be curious about the process. Ask lots of questions.

❓ Questions to Ask

- What is going on in this process? What are all the reasons for the variation?
- Do I like the current level? If everything were right, at what level would the process be operating? What is the gap between the current level and the desired level? How much is the cost of the gap and what should be done?

- Has there been a process shift?
- Has anything changed? Is the change in the right direction?
- Is the change the one I expected?
- Do I know the causes for the change?
- Does this process have a cycle or a pattern to it?
- Are any trends showing up? Do I know what the causes are?
- Are things getting better? Or worse?
- Should I translate this chart into a statistical control chart?
- What other charts do I need to understand what is going on?

! Points to Remember

- A run chart always shows what happens *over a time period*. Make sure the data is plotted in time ordered sequence.
- Time or sequence is shown on the horizontal axis and count or measurement is on the vertical axis. Be sure to label the chart completely so anyone can read it.
- Annotate the chart with other information such as process changes and other contributing factors which will help the reader understand what is happening.
- Update the chart regularly. Use it as a basis for understanding and improvement.
- Choose the right thing to measure. Don't use quantity alone when percent would be more meaningful. Measure characteristics that are important to the customer.
- What you choose to chart reflects what you believe is important. Chart only those things that matter most to the quality and productivity of an important process.

Pareto Chart

A Pareto chart is a simple bar graph ranking in order of importance the causes, sources, types or reasons for problems and/or opportunities. It helps to determine what to work on.

The Pareto chart is a visual tool for prioritization. Pareto charts are commonly used to classify problems in service, manufacturing, or administrative processes and to compare costs or dollars associated with the work. Gathering data about troubles, problems and opportunities focuses attention on those things that need to be changed to eliminate the waste. Since you cannot work effectively on all sources of waste or opportunity at the same time, you need to set priorities.

The *Pareto Principle* states that 80% of the effects you are interested in are caused by 20% of the underlying factors. Therefore, you will be most effective if you work first on the *Vital Few* things that will yield the biggest improvements, rather than be distracted by the **less important many.** The "right" things to work on could be those things that occur most frequently, cost the most, are easiest to do, will have the biggest impact on customer satisfaction, etc. This principle applies to invoice errors, customer complaints, estimated sales from new product opportunities, anything that involves work and is important to you.

The following chart shows that shipping errors are by far the most frequently occurring defect. Working to eliminate shipping errors should probably be the top priority for reducing customer complaints. It will be more valuable to the organization and may be easier to reduce shipping errors by one half than to eliminate pricing complaints entirely.

Customer Complaints - November

# of Complaints (y-axis)

Complaint Type: Shipping, Invoice Error, Pricing, Delivery, Quality, Other

The Pareto chart is a way of ranking any problem or opportunity with the best information you have. Although it is desirable to work from hard data, you can use estimates or opinions, such as estimated sales for new products.

> **The Pareto Principle** is of utmost importance in continuous improvement. You need to work on the right things to succeed. The world is full of people working very hard, but on the wrong things. The Pareto Principle tells you to always work on the **Vital Few** things that will really make a difference. Who needs the Pareto chart? Everyone! It helps you make good decisions. The most important decision you make each day is what to work on. Who needs the Pareto Principle the most? Top managers! The higher up you are—the more you need it.
>
> William E. Conway

Making a Pareto Chart

Pick an important area of waste/opportunity and decide how to measure the various contributors—number of defects, number of errors, pounds of waste, dollars spent, sales dollars, time taken, etc.

- Gather the data. Use recent historical data or set up a check sheet to collect the data needed. Use a certain time period or production quantity from which to gather the data such as one shift, one day, one week, or 1000 units of production, 3000 pounds, etc. You should have at least thirty items. You can make a chart with fewer, if necessary, but it will be less representative.

- Count the frequency or quantity of each type, cause, reason or source. Arrange or number them in descending order from largest to smallest.

- Construct a bar graph with the quantity or units of measure shown on the vertical axis. Make it tall enough to accommodate the largest bar you will have. Along the horizontal axis list the category with the largest numerical value on the left followed by the other categories in descending order of frequency or quantity. Draw a bar (column) for each cause with the height representing the frequency or quantity of that cause. Items which occur very infrequently can be lumped in an "other" category at the far right.

- It is sometimes helpful to add a line showing the cumulative percent of causes. That is, what percentage of the total does the first cause represent? The first two? The first three? A second scale is added to the right-hand side of the chart to measure percent. Since it represents 100% of the causes, its height is equal to the total number of causes in all categories. This is a useful way to see if the 80-20 principle applies to your area of study.

Customer Complaints - November

Here 50% of the defects are from the first cause, 80% from the first two causes, etc. This information helps put in perspective how many items would be effective to work on.

Using the Pareto Chart

Pareto charts are more than just a tool. They represent a way of thinking, the Pareto mentality. The Pareto mentality keeps you working on the most important items. Pareto charts are also useful in evaluating opportunities as well as problems. For example, a Pareto chart might help decide how to allocate engineering effort to new products.

Potential Gross Margin $ from New Products

$ (000)

New Products Under Development

This chart could help in the allocation of limited resources.

Notice that the opportunities are measured in gross margin dollars, not in sales dollars. A chart in sales dollars might be misleading, since the product with the most sales potential might not be the most profitable. An even better measure might be net profit dollars, if that were reasonable to estimate.

Note: It is often better to measure the cost or benefit of each item in money rather than units. For example, in a chart of defects, some categories may be reworked at low cost, other rework may cost more, and some types of defects must be scrapped. For safety incidents, cuts may be the most frequently occurring injury, but a few back or repetitive work injuries can be far more costly. In a supermarket, some canned goods with a dent can be sold at full price. Other dents require a special sale; still others must be discarded. Thus a chart of numbers of defects alone may be misleading.

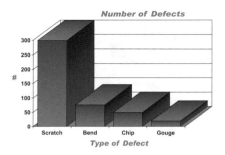

If you change this to the estimated cost of defects, you get a very different picture.

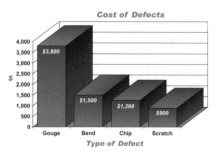

Since gouges cause a piece to be scrapped, they are the most costly, though the least frequent, defect. Scratches, which cost little to rework, turn out to be the least important source of dollar loss. Units alone can be misleading. Use a financial measure whenever practical. Notice how this chart displays the value of each bar. This labeling often provides a better grasp of the relative values of each bar.

Often when you start to work on the first one or two bars of a Pareto chart you find that you need more detailed information. For example, if you are working on customer complaints, you may discover there are several different causes for customer complaints. If this is a significant area of waste, you should identify and measure the causes of complaints, and make a Pareto chart for those causes. For example:

Then there may be sub-causes of the two major causes which will require two more Pareto charts.

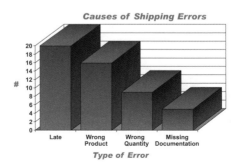

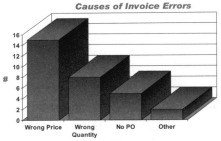

Causes of Invoice Errors

Type of Error

More charts may be needed to discover the causes of the wrong product being shipped or the wrong price on the invoice. Go down as many levels as necessary to discover the fundamental causes. When you dig deeply enough into the work, it usually becomes obvious what to do to fix the problem.

Use Pareto charts for your own work every day to continually evaluate what is most important to accomplish. It helps avoid the waste of spending time on minor problems while neglecting the important ones. Even when you don't draw a Pareto chart, visualize one for every area of your activity. This "Pareto mentality" is a characteristic of people who really make a difference.

? Questions to Ask

- Do you have recent Pareto charts associated with your most important processes?
- Are you using the right measurement?
- Over what period of time is the data charted? Is that enough information to be representative

of the process? If you made a Pareto chart of the same information for a different time period, how would it compare?

- What additional Pareto charts do you need to make to decide what to work on? Have you considered frequency, time, cost, ease of doing, resources required or customer impact in making your decision?
- Do you need to make sub-Pareto charts of each bar to narrow the scope of the problem or opportunity?
- Do you have the Pareto mentality? Are you always trying to find and quantify the **Vital Few** things to work on—the things which promise the most benefit?
- Are you taking action for improvement as a result of your Pareto charts?
- Are you using Pareto charts as a communication tool?

Points to Remember

- Arrange the bars in descending order, except for the category "other" which is placed at the far right.
- Use the Pareto mentality to decide what to work on. Consider frequency, cost, time, ease, customer impact, etc. in your decision.
- Study the major categories and make a sub-Pareto chart to understand the process better. Use the other simple tools to supplement your understanding.
- Keep breaking down the causes further and further until what to do becomes obvious.

Flow Chart

A flow chart is a map of a process. It is used to identify the actual or ideal sequence of steps in a process, identify waste, plan improvements and standardize the work. It also serves as a communication and training tool to help everyone visualize the process in the same way.

A flow chart can be made with varying degrees of detail depending on how you plan to use it. The simplest type, a **block flow**, shows the sequence of major steps in the process. It contains limited detail and is a good starting point, but never the final step.

Making A Sale

```
┌──────────┐    ┌──────────┐    ┌──────────┐
│ Identify │ →  │ Contact  │ →  │  Close   │
│ Prospect │    │ Customer │    │   Sale   │
└──────────┘    └──────────┘    └──────────┘
```

This broad overview of the selling process could be used to begin a discussion.

A **top down flow chart** shows main steps of the

Plan The Meeting	Carry Out The Meeting	Follow-up On The Meeting
• Define purpose & desired outcomes • Identify participants • Design agenda • Secure meeting space • Notify participants & send agenda	• Review agenda & ground rules • Clarify roles & responsibilities • Work through agenda • Identify action items, responsibilities & time frames • Plan next agenda & meeting time • Process check	• Send minutes • Check in re: action items - provide help as required • Keep others informed

process in blocks arranged horizontally across the top of the page with major sub-steps listed below. It is helpful to keep main steps and sub-steps to less than 10 each.

The **macro flow chart** shows a greater level of detail than the block or top down flow charts.

It also:

- shows basic steps
- shows decision points
- shows recycle loops
- shows work and wait times
- highlights problems/opportunities
- shows where to measure variation

The most common flow charts show more detailed steps with an estimated time for each step and the total elapsed time. If the process is unusually complex, the flow chart may be even more detailed. Each step may be broken down further into sub-steps to the degree of detail needed. Additional information such cost per step, staffing, etc. may be added as needed.

The micro flow chart shows the greatest level of process detail. It also shows all components of the process cycle time. Symbols denote the type of activity that the process step represents.

Making a Flow Chart

Standard flow charting symbols are used as a common language to indicate the type of activity each step represents; six conventional symbols are usually sufficient.

The Symbols	Denotes	Examples
Diamond ◆	Decision	· is the part good? · is the supplier the right one?
Square ■	Control/ Inspection	· verify travel requisition · check time cards · inspect part · approve salary increase
Circle ●	Operation	· make a copy · type a memo · run the machine · interview applicant
Arrow ➡	Movement/ Transfer	· send data to mainframe · deliver material to next work station · transport goods to customer · walking/shipping
"D" ▶	Delay	· waiting time (for response, in line, for instructions) · down time
Triangle ▼	File	· file document, copy a disk.

- Give the process a title and describe its inputs and outputs, its suppliers and customers.

- Decide on the boundaries. Boundaries are the start and end points of the process to be studied. Which operations will be included? Which operations will be excluded?

- How much detail will be appropriate?

- Gather data, documenting all of the steps in the process. Observe the process and/or talk to the people involved. If it is a new process being planned, a group discussion to visualize the process is helpful. The following form may be used to gather the data. The example shows how an order is processed in a small distribution center.

Process Flow Chart Data Collection

Present Method

___ **Proposed Method**

Subject Charted: _Processing an order_

Department: _____

Date: 2/26

Chart by: RCH

Chart #: 2

Sheet _1_ of _1_

Time in Minutes	Chart Symbols	Process Description
4	●⊏▷□◇D▽	Receive order by phone, fax, e-mail or mail
5	●⊏▷□◇D▽	Write phone order onto form
3	O⊏▷■◇D▽	Check fax, e-mail and mail orders for errors
1	O⊏▷□◆D▽	Order correct?
6	●⊏▷□◇D▽	Contact customer
4	●⊏▷□◇D▽	Price order
3	●⊏▷□◇D▽	Make copy of order
2	O⊏▷□◇D▼	File original
3	●⊏▷□◇D▽	Check credit limits
4	●⊏▷□◇D▽	Enter order in computer
2	O▶□◇D▽	Send order copy to warehouse
80	O⊏▷□◇●▽	Wait for return of order copy from warehouse
1	O⊏▷□◆D▽	Order complete?
3	●⊏▷□◇D▽	Modify order to show backorder
2	●⊏▷□◇D▽	Print out shipping documents
2	O▶□◇D▽	Send shipping documents to warehouse
2	●⊏▷□◇D▽	Print out invoice
2	O⊏▷□◇D▼	File invoice in pending file to await shipment
	O⊏▷□◇D▽	
	O⊏▷□◇D▽	
	O⊏▷□◇D▽	
	O⊏▷□◇D▽	
	O⊏▷□◇D▽	
	O⊏▷□◇D▽	
	O⊏▷□◇D▽	

- Draw the flow chart from the information on the data collection sheet using the charting symbols. Connect the symbols with lines showing the direction of the work flow.

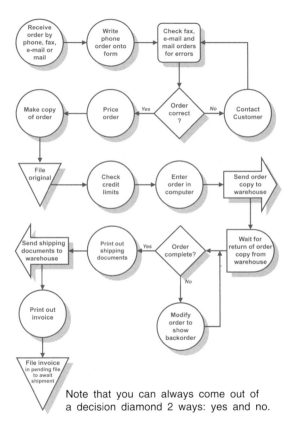

Note that you can always come out of a decision diamond 2 ways: yes and no.

- Review the chart for accuracy. Make revisions if needed.

- Make a Pareto chart showing the time spent on the various types of activities.

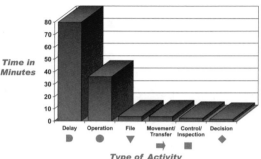

- Search for waste. Imagine the perfect process. Look at all the steps, such as delays, which do not add value and try to find a way to reduce or eliminate them. Can you change, rearrange, combine or simplify to improve the process?

- Identify specific areas for improvement (rework loops, delays, multiple inspections or authorizations, etc.)

- Collect data about numbers of occurrences and reasons for rework or other problems.

- Make sub-process flow charts to break the work into finer pieces as necessary to understand the process fully.

- Draw a new chart with the modifications you want, discuss it with the people involved, and test it.

Analyzing The Flow Chart

- Is this how the process really works?

- What are the obvious problems?

- Which could be fixed immediately?

- Where is the waste?

- How long does this process take?

- What would the process look like if it were perfect?

- What steps are not value added?

- Which steps can be eliminated, improved, combined, rearranged or simplified?

Look for the non-value added steps or those which can be improved, combined or rearranged.

Compare the process time to cycle time - get rid of the wait/dead time.

To add more information to a process flow chart and convert it to a process map, include the inputs and outputs at each step. **Inputs** are key process variables required to perform the step. They are known as x's and can include people, methods, materials, equipment, measurements and environment. **Outputs** are the key result variables of the process step. Outputs are shown as y's. Outputs include goods, services, measurements or consequences.

? Questions to Ask

Eliminate
- Does each step add value?
- Is there duplication?
- Can you eliminate delays? Inspection steps? Filing steps?
- Are some operations rework?

Change
- How can the operation be changed? Different methods? Technology? Equipment?
- Less costly material or service?
- Reduce the frequency of the service?
- The # of people receiving the service?
- Reduce the time it takes?

Rearrange
- Is the layout the most efficient?
- Can you eliminate transport steps?
- Is the sequence the most efficient?

Combine
- Can any operations be combined? With a supplier's operation? With a customer's?

Simplify
- What is the simplest way to achieve the objective(s) of the process?
- Are instructions easy to understand?

Imagine – visualize the process with no waste
- What would the perfect process look like?
- How much time would it take?
- How much would it cost?
- How would it affect customer satisfaction? employee or associate satisfaction? the business?

! Points to Remember

- Start with a simple chart and add detail as needed.
- Classify the activities using the six symbols.
- The people doing the work should chart the process.
- Make a Pareto chart of the categories of activity. Try to eliminate delays and work that do not add value.
- Collect data and display it in other charts to understand the process.
- Draw an imagineered chart based on the way you think the process should work.
- Compare the differences. Quantify the value of the changes.
- Make the changes.

Fishbone Chart

A fishbone chart (also known as a cause and effect or Ishikawa diagram) shows relationships between causes and a particular effect you want to study. It is used to identify potential causes and root causes of problems or opportunities. The major categories of causes contributing to the effect are assigned to the main branches of the diagram. Gather the "experts" (the people who know the most about the work) then brainstorm all of the possible causes of that effect.

A simple fishbone chart looks something like the skeleton of a fish.

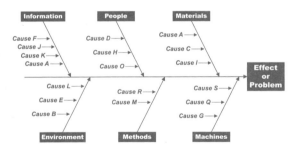

The chart usually becomes more complex with the addition of sub-causes for many of the prime causes. It begins to resemble a tree lying on its side with main branches, sub-branches, sub-sub branches, twigs, sub-twigs, etc. Sometimes a critical or fundamental cause may be found on a sub-twig.

The six categories of causes shown (people, materials, machines, methods, information and environment are relevant in most situations. Measurement is also often appropriate. Use whatever makes sense for the particular effect. Usually, three to six categories are enough. Sometimes the steps in a process (e.g., drill, machine, input data, assemble, test) are used to classify causes. When analyzing administrative processes, "policies" and "procedures" may be useful major categories. Any major categories are suitable if they help people think creatively about what the cause of the effect might be.

Making and Using a Fishbone Chart

Decide what problem or opportunity to study. Clearly define this effect and place it in a box on the right side of your diagram.

- Gather people that have knowledge of, or experience with, the effect you are studying. Try to get a diverse group so that they will have different perspectives. Although an individual can create a fishbone chart, a group generates many more ideas for possible causes.

- Appoint a leader and a scribe. The leader should encourage a brainstorming atmosphere with free flowing ideas and a minimum of ground rules.

Brainstorming Ground Rules

Clearly state the idea to be brainstormed

Brainstorm individually (write down ideas silently)

Group brainstorm:
- *Record all ideas accurately*
- *One idea per turn, use round robin*
- *No criticizing or commenting*
- *No idea is "too wild"*
- *Piggy back on others' ideas*
- *It is okay to pass*

Review each idea:
- *For understanding and clarification*
- *To combine and eliminate*

- Try to have everyone contribute ideas about possible causes. Remember, only causes, not solutions! The scribe writes down the causes as they are suggested. The scribe can write the causes on a fishbone, but it may be difficult to classify them properly without slowing the flow of ideas. An effective way to avoid this problem is to write each idea on a Post-it™ note and construct the fishbone later by posting the notes in the appropriate place. A sample fishbone from one such group is shown on the next page.

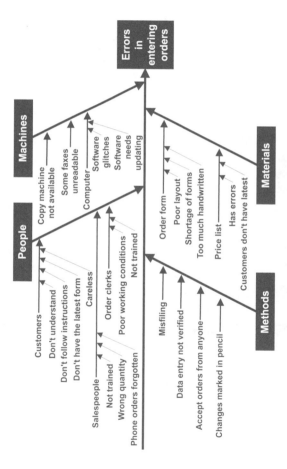

Errors in entering orders

Machines
- Copy machine not available
- Some faxes unreadable
- Computer
  - Software glitches
  - Software needs updating

People
- Customers
  - Don't understand
  - Don't follow instructions
  - Don't have the latest form
- Careless
- Order clerks
  - Poor working conditions
  - Not trained
- Salespeople
  - Not trained
  - Wrong quantity
  - Phone orders forgotten

Materials
- Order form
  - Poor layout
  - Shortage of forms
  - Too much handwritten
- Price list
  - Has errors
  - Customers don't have latest

Methods
- Misfiling
- Data entry not verified
- Accept orders from anyone
- Changes marked in pencil

57

- Rank the causes for further study. Pick several that the group thinks will have the greatest impact on the problem or opportunity being studied. Use either consensus or a vote. Fix the obvious right away.

- Now that you have priorities, you will probably need more hard facts. Assign team members to gather data. Solicit help from people outside the group where appropriate.

- Review the data. Make a Pareto chart of the major causes. Determine whether priorities need to be changed and update the chart with any new information. Put the fishbone chart in a final form, highlight the major causes and distribute to participants. Consider placing the chart in a common area such as on a bulletin board or a shared drive as a way of soliciting further ideas.

- Consider the use of the "Effect-Cause-Effect" diagram to eliminate possible causes which do not explain the observed effect. For example, if the car won't start, a possible cause is a dead battery. If the battery is dead, other observed effects include no dome lights, power locks don't work, etc. If the dome light does in fact work, then you know that a dead battery is not a possible cause and can be eliminated from further consideration.

- Determine which major causes to work on.

- For each of the major causes, ask "Why?" five times to try to identify a root or fundamental cause.

? Questions to Ask

- Is the problem or opportunity being studied an important one?
- Is it clearly defined? Do the people developing the fishbone understand the problem?
- Do the major cause categories help people think creatively about all the possible causes of the issue?
- Does the atmosphere make people feel free to contribute their ideas?
- Do all the causes fit logically under one of the branches of the fishbone, or should there be another branch(es)?
- Have you asked "Why?" five times for each of the major factors?
- What additional data is needed to verify and attack each of the major causes?
- Would it be helpful to convert the data into a Pareto chart or a run chart?

! Points to Remember

- Categories represent the major elements/ contributors to the problem, process or opportunity.
- The most common categories for a fishbone are people, materials, methods, machines, information and environment.
- Involve people who know various aspects of the process. Specialists outside the process may also help.
- Brainstorm only causes, not solutions.
- Delve deeply into the causes by asking "Why?" five times.
- A fishbone represents opinions. Opinions must be verified with facts before action to change is taken.

Histogram

A histogram is a frequency distribution which shows the variation produced by a process. It can also be used to show the capability of a process.

A histogram is a bar graph that shows how often a measurement occurs over the range of measurements the process produces. The spread of the variation, where it is centered and the shape of the distribution provide clues about how the process is operating. It gives you a "snapshot" of how your process is operating.

Below is an example of a histogram of the time between receipt and shipment of an order for Warehouse A.

Warehouse A - Days to Ship
(534 Orders)

This chart shows that most items are shipped in 3 or 4 days. The average time it takes to ship an order is 3.45 days. If the company's objective is to ship all orders within 4 days, the average time alone does not provide enough information for the company to know whether it is meeting its objective. But the histogram reveals that about 80 orders, or 15% of the total, are shipped late. This information gives an idea of the size of the problem and some idea of what needs to be done to fix it. For this sample histogram, the data is counted (# of days to ship).

When the data is measured, the graph might look something like this one showing the length of a sample of metal rods produced in a process.

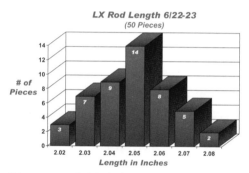

In this case each label shows the midpoint of the measurements represented by that bar.

Constructing a Histogram
The simplest way to construct a histogram is from a check sheet. To construct a chart of rod lengths like the one shown above, set up a check sheet and begin measuring.

- Count the number of data points in the data set (n).

- Determine the range (R) for the data set. The range is the difference in the value between the largest value and the smallest value.

- Divide the range into classes (K). The number of classes or bars depends on how many measurements or data points you have. Use the following as a guide to determine the number of classes.

Number of Data (n)	Number of Classes (K)
Under 50	5-7
50-100	6-10
100-250	7-12
Over 250	10-20

In this case, you plan 50 data points and your judgment from past history is that the range of measurements will be from about 2.015" to 2.085" or a range of .070". Assume you can measure to the nearest .001 inch. With 50 measurements you might choose 7 classes or bars to portray the dispersion of data—the variation in the process.

- Determine the class width (H). One formula often used is $H = R/K$. Depending upon the data, you can round off to determine class width. In this case divide the range, .07, by the number of desired classes, 7, and get .01. If your calculation gives a number such as .0086, it would be convenient to round up to .01 as the class interval.

- Label each bar with the midpoint or the range of the class it represents. Be sure that intervals are mutually exclusive so that data points will be properly recorded.

Check Sheet

Date: 8/26   **Product:** LX Rods
Machine: 23   **Shift:** 1st

			X			
			X			
			X			
			X			
			X			
		X	X			
		X	X	X		
	X	X	X	X		
	X	X	X	X		
	X	X	X	X	X	
	X	X	X	X	X	
X	X	X	X	X	X	
X	X	X	X	X	X	X
X	X	X	X	X	X	X
2.02	2.03	2.04	2.05	2.06	2.07	2.08

- The completed check sheet resembles a histogram.

- Transfer this picture to a histogram. You can do this by making a bar to enclose each class of x's and then erasing the x's.

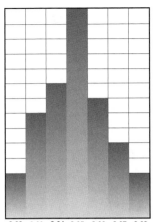

2.02 2.03 2.04 2.05 2.06 2.07 2.08

You can approximate a curve with the amount of data you have. If you took more and more readings and added more and more classes, the difference in the bar heights would become smaller until the histogram eventually became a curve.

- Another type of check sheet is sometimes used, particularly when you have a large amount of data.

Class	Midpoint
2.015 - <2.025	111
2.025 - <2.035	~~1111~~ 11
2.035 - <2.045	~~1111~~ 1111
2.045 - <2.055	~~1111~~ ~~1111~~ 1111
2.055 - <2.065	~~1111~~ 111
2.065 - <2.075	~~1111~~
2.075 - <2.085	11

Notice that the shape of the accumulated tick marks is the same as that of the histogram lying on its side.

Using a Histogram

The histogram gives a good picture of the central tendency (average) of the data and the dispersion (variation). It also shows the range of the measurements, the difference between the highest and the lowest count or measure, which defines the **process capability**. By adding customer specifications to the histogram, you can determine if the process is capable. A process is capable when all of the data points produced by it fall within the customer specifications.

Indicating the number of occurrences at the top of each bar sometimes makes the chart easier to use.

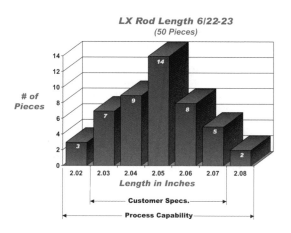

The histogram shows that the process capability is 2.015" - 2.085" and the range is .070".

Let's assume that the customer specification for the length of the piece is 2.050" +/- .025". This means the customer will accept bars between 2.025" and 2.075" long, a range of .050". The process made five pieces outside these dimensions; 10% of the fifty-piece lot is out of specifications.

You need to improve the process to insure it can meet customer specifications 100% of the time. Brainstorm all the reasons for excessive variation in the process.

Then collect data and identify what must be improved to reduce the spread of the variation permanently. This may require more operator training, machine adjustment, more frequent tool changes, a different fixture for holding the bar, etc.

The histogram can tell you other things. For example, in this chart, undersize pieces occur somewhat more frequently than oversize pieces. This may give you a clue as to what is happening. After changes in the process are made, new histograms can tell you about any progress.

The shape of the histogram can provide other clues as to what is happening in the process. We would expect that any process which is repeated over time and for which there is an equal likelihood of data points falling above and below the average will tend to exhibit a normal distribution with a bell-shaped curve.

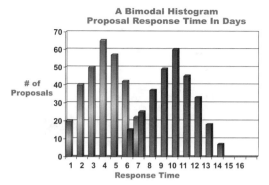

A Bimodal Histogram
Proposal Response Time In Days

# of Proposals

Response Time

This bimodal histogram is sometimes called a "camel" because it shows two humps or peaks. This shape reflects two different processes, such as output from two different offices, two shifts, or two similar machines. Segregate the data by the two processes and make two histograms. Then investigate the causes for the differences and try to improve one or both processes.

When the histogram appears to end abruptly on one side it is sometimes called cliff-like. This may be caused when the minimum value at the "cliff" is zero. When the minimum is not zero, it is likely that some of the items below the "cliff" have been removed by inspection because they did not meet specifications. You may have a "cliff" on either side or both sides of a distribution. This kind of distribution from a supplier indicates the supplier's process is not capable of meeting specifications and is generating waste. If the supplier's item is important, it may be worthwhile to work with the supplier to improve the process capability and reduce the waste, or to examine your specifications to see if they can be changed.

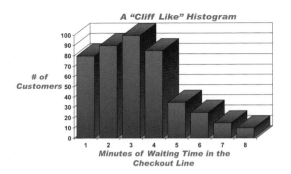

A "Cliff Like" Histogram

# of Customers

Minutes of Waiting Time in the Checkout Line

? Questions to Ask

- What is the shape of the histogram? Is it symmetrical? Is it a "camel"? Cliff-like? Skewed to one side or the other?
- What does the shape tell about the process? Does it show a normal distribution? If it does not, why not?
- What is the range of the data? How does the range compare with the specifications? Is the process capable? Will it still be capable if the process drifts?
- How much improvement is necessary? Possible? What can you do to narrow the range?
- Does the target value for the process coincide with the highest bar? With the average? If not, what must you do to shift the process toward the target?
- Would other tools be helpful? Fishbone? Run chart? Pareto chart?

❗ Points to Remember

- A histogram is useful for data that is either counted or measured.
- Data can be entered on a check sheet. Gather at least 50 data points. More points may make it more accurate and meaningful.
- A histogram shows process capability when compared to customer specifications.
- After process changes, a new histogram is useful for showing progress.

Correlation Chart

A correlation chart is a scatter plot which shows how one variable changes in relation to another. It is used to discover and document possible cause and effect.

The correlation chart is used to test for a possible relationship between two variables and to show the strength of that relationship. Often there are a number of potential causes for process variation and it is important to determine which of the causes have the most effect on (correlation with) the outcome. *Showing a relationship between two variables does not prove cause and effect.* A third cause may affect both variables. Use common sense to determine whether an apparent cause and effect relationship is logical.

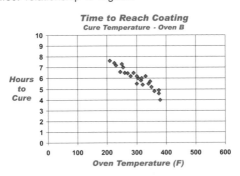

Time to Reach Coating
Cure Temperature - Oven B

In this example it appears logical that the coating cures in a shorter time with a hotter oven, just as a roast cooks faster in a hotter oven. There may be other factors, such as chemical composition of the coating, which would also affect cure time. In this case the cure time and the oven temperature show a negative correlation, that is, as the oven temperature goes up, the time to cure goes down. In a positive correlation, one variable increases as the other increases. For example, most of the time a person's weight correlates positively with their height.

The points on the time vs. temperature chart form almost a straight line, indicating a strong correlation. Within the range of temperature shown, an increase in the temperature produces a nearly proportionate decrease in the cure time. On the other hand, a chart of weight vs. height is not so strongly correlated, because other factors, such as eating habits, exercise and bone structure, affect weight.

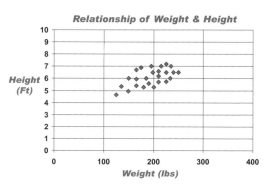

Relationship of Weight & Height

Correlation charts are most useful when you are uncertain what is causing the variation in a process, whether service, manufacturing or scientific. Using a chart to test the correlation of various factors can help pinpoint the most crucial factors.

Making a Correlation Chart

Pick two factors to test their correlation. Since correlation most often implies cause and effect, pick a factor that you are trying to control or change (the effect). Then pick a second factor (the cause) that you believe makes the first factor vary.

- Gather data in pairs. Assume you are concerned about how fast drill bits are wearing out and want to determine the effect of cutting speed on the life of the drill bits.

Pair #	Cutting Speed (inches/minute)	Bit Life (minutes)
1	0.9	33
2	1.3	22
3	1.1	25
etc.		
*		
*		
50	0.8	47

Try to gather at least 50, but no more than 100 pairs of data.

- Prepare a chart with X and Y axes. Plot the expected cause (cutting speed) on the X or horizontal axis, and the effect (bit life) on the Y or vertical axis. For ease of reading the two, axes should be about the same length.

- Plot each data pair as a point on the chart. If more than one pair falls at the same point, draw one or more circles around the point as needed.

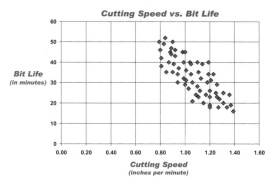

Cutting Speed vs. Bit Life

Bit Life (in minutes)

Cutting Speed (inches per minute)

This chart can help to pick out the optimum speed for this cutting operation. Obviously bit life is only one of the factors to be considered. Other factors would be time to change bits, cost of drill bits, defects caused by burnt bits, etc.

The correlation chart is most useful when a number of variables may affect the outcome of a process. By charting each variable against the outcome or effect, we can see if, and to what degree, the two factors are related. Relationship does not necessarily mean cause and effect, because the variation in both factors may be caused by a third, yet-to-be-measured factor. Usually common sense will tell you whether one factor is actually causing the other. The degree of correlation can be determined roughly by looking at the chart or with regression analysis.

The closer the pattern of dots is to a straight line, the stronger the correlation. A completely random pattern indicates no correlation. A weak correlation indicates other factors are also affecting one or both variables.

? Questions to Ask

- Have you identified the most important variables affecting the outcome of the process?
- Is there a cause and effect relationship between the variables charted, or is a third factor causing the variation in both?
- If the correlation is weak, what other factors are involved?
- How can you improve the *cause* to get the desired *effect*?

! Points to Remember

- A correlation chart will show if there is a relationship between two variables and the strength of that relationship.
- The closer the chart is to a straight line, the stronger the relationship.
- Use it when you want to determine what the effect of changing one variable in a process will be on another variable.

Control Chart

A control chart is a run chart that plots data in order as it occurs and that also displays upper and lower control limits which are calculated from the data. It can be used to sort random from non-random variation as a basis for analyzing, improving, stabilizing, and controlling the process.

The control chart tells you how your process is doing currently, how stable or predictable it is, what type of variation is occurring and how capable it is.

This chart takes the two key parameters of a histogram ($\bar{X}$ - the average and R - the range of data) and plots them over time. Statistical formulas are used to plot control limits on the chart.

Data Collection Sheet

	8:00	8:15	8:30	8:45	9:00	9:15	9:30	9:45	10:00
	299	315	322	289	328	309	327	316	312
	305	294	311	312	323	301	306	319	305
	315	331	322	325	314	308	321	317	321
	288	325	304	298	290	297	296	298	308
	310	302	320	303	297	300	301	312	297
Total	1517	1567	1579	1527	1552	1515	1551	1562	1543
Average	303.4	313.4	315.8	305.4	310.4	303	310.2	312.4	308.6
Range	27	37	18	36	38	12	31	21	24

$$\bar{\bar{X}} = 309.2$$
$$UCL\bar{X} = 324.5$$
$$LCL\bar{X} = 293.9$$
$$\bar{R} = 27.1$$
$$UCL\bar{R} = 57.32$$
$$LCL\bar{R} = 0$$

Control limits indicate the range of variation inherent in the way the process runs. Data outside those limits indicate "special causes" which are not part of the normal process. These need to be investigated and eliminated to achieve a stable process with a known range of variation. This stability means the process is predictable. Stability is necessary before the control chart can be used to control and improve the process.

Making a Control Chart

As in all studies of work processes, the most important step is deciding what factor to study. The control chart is most frequently used in repetitive operations which are important to the organization and for which data can be made available. It is useful for understanding and improving any process including management, planning, and sales.

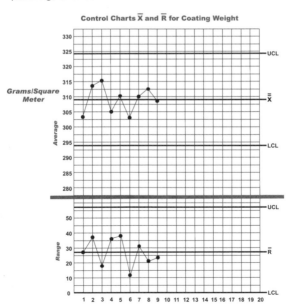

Control Charts $\overline{X}$ and $\overline{R}$ for Coating Weight

Some detailed study and/or training is needed to construct and interpret control charts. Some useful reminders for those who have been trained follows:

For factors which are measured rather than counted, (i.e., length, weight, density, etc.) Use an $\bar{X}$-$\bar{R}$ chart.

$$\bar{X} \text{ control limits} = \bar{\bar{X}} \pm A_2 \bar{R}$$

$$\bar{R} \text{ control limits} = D_4 \bar{R} \text{ and } D_3 \bar{R}$$

The following chart shows the value of the three factors for different sample sizes. The sample size is represented by "n".

"n"	A_2	D_4	D_3
1	2.660		
2	1.880	3.267	0
3	1.023	2.575	0
4	0.729	2.282	0
5	0.577	2.115	0
6	0.483	2.004	0
7	0.419	1.924	0.076

Other types of control charts include:

np for factors which are counted, such as number defective

p for fraction defective

c for number of defects in a fixed unit of product, such as surface imperfections in auto fenders of constant size

u for number of defects when the material being examined is not constant in size such as pieces of facbric

Control limits for these charts can be calculated
by adding and subtracting from the average:

Average	±3 times the square root of	Divided by the square root of
np	$np(1-p)$	-
p	$\bar{p}(1-p)$	n
c	$\bar{c}$	-
u	$\bar{u}$	n

Using Control Charts

The control chart has four main functions—to
analyze, stabilize, control and improve a process.
The control chart can tell you whether a process is
stable (in statistical control) and the limits within
which it actually operates (its capability). To test
for stability, plot a control chart of the variable
selected (100 or more data points, when possible).
Then plot it again at a later period. If there are no
points outside the control limits, and if the average
and range of the two trials are approximately the
same, you can conclude that the process is stable.
That is, it will give predictable results. The
variation is inherent in the process itself, a result of
"common" causes, with no "special" or unusual
causes of variation.

- If the process is not in statistical control, it is
  not stable. Use the control chart to help track
  down the reasons for special causes and for
  any significant changes in the average or
  range of operation.

- Once the process is stable, the control chart
  can be used to keep the process in control
  and maintain that stability. By plotting the
  results of a process as they occur, an operator

can determine if any special causes are affecting the process or if the process itself is drifting—if there is a change in average and/or range. The control chart is "the voice of the process" providing you with signals when changes are taking place. The most common signal of change is a point falling outside the control limits. The chart is saying **"Something unusual has happened that is not a part of the process. You should investigate."** Other tests for process changes are also valuable.

- To use these tests, first divide the control chart into six equal "zones", three on each side of the average line.

The first two tests show a strong probability that the average is shifting for some reason.

Eight points in a row increasing or decreasing

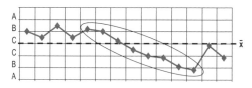

Eight points in a row on one side of the center line

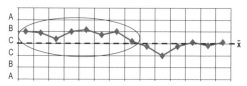

If fourteen points in a row alternating up and down it indicates a periodic shift in the process, or perhaps that data are being drawn from two different processes.

Fourteen points in a row alternating up and down

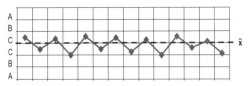

If you need an early warning that special causes may be present, two more sensitive tests are available. These may give a false signal in two cases out of a hundred.

Two out of three points in a row in zone A

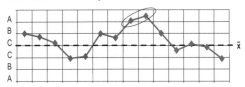

Four out of five points in a row in zone B or beyond

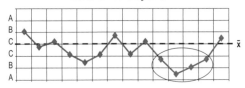

To use these tests to control a process, plot the data as soon as it is practical. This allows a quick reaction to process problems. It also makes it easier to identify the cause of a problem, because the control chart can signal a problem on a near real-time basis.

Since a control chart shows the average and range of process operation, it can be used to check for improvement. It is sometimes difficult to see the effect of a change in the process because it may be hidden by random variation. By plotting a control chart before and after the change, you can get an accurate picture of any improvement in the average level and any narrowing or widening of the range. This information is valuable in experimenting with process changes.

❓ Questions to Ask

- What is the key variable(s)?
- Is it important to see when the process changes?
- What type of control chart is appropriate for the data?
- Is the process stable? If not, what needs to be done to stabilize it?
- Is the control chart being kept on a real-time basis? By the process operator?
- What action should be taken when special causes appear? Stop the process? Call the supervisor? Call an engineer?
- Can the operator give any clues as to a special cause(s)?
- Does the average level need to be changed and/or the range narrowed?

❗ Points to Remember

- A process must be stable before you can use a control chart effectively for improvement.
- Use 25 or more data points to calculate control limits.
- Plot points on a control chart as soon as practical to discover problems quickly.
- Compute a new average and range after making process changes. This will tell you what the change(s) did to the process.
- Just because a process is stable and predictable does not mean it meets customer requirements.
- For any out of control point on the control chart, record the reason for it and the action taken.

Process Capability

Think of customer requirements as a "gate" through which the output of a process must pass. The customer defines the sides or limits of the gate by what range of variation is acceptable. These are called the specification limits. The capability of the process to meet those specifications is determined by the stability of the process, the range of variation, and the process aim point or target.

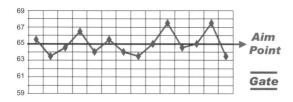

The graph represents a stable process, but one which has the wrong aim point, and too wide a range.

A stable process operates within a predictable range, and therefore is said to be "in statistical control" (see control charts). It does not display unpredictable, special causes of variation. The variation in a stable process is inherent in the process itself. The more you are able to reduce the normal variation in a process, the more "elbow room" you have to meet customer specifications should the process drift. It is impossible to insure meeting specifications at all times if the output of the process is unstable and/or unpredictable. Each special cause of variation must be tracked down, identified and eliminated on a permanent basis.

In the process shown above the customer specifications or "gate" for the power used by a light bulb might be 60 watts, with a variation allowed from 59 to 61 watts. The actual process shown is making bulbs with an aim point or average of 65 watts, and a variation from 62.5 to 67.5 watts. None of the output will go through the customer's "gate".

The process for making the bulbs must be adjusted to bring the aim point down to near the center of the gate, or 60 watts.

Assume the aim point is now the center of the gate. Some of the process output will meet customer specifications, but not all. The range of process variation is still too much. With no reduction in variation the output will vary from 57.5 watts to 62.5 watts. (At this point, some suppliers will inspect and sort those that meet customer specifications and those that don't.)

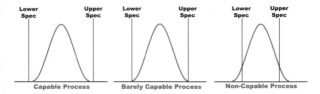

The next step is to identify and reduce some of the causes of variation inherent in the process–the common causes. If you can reduce the range of the process output to plus or minus 1 watt around the aim point, you will have a process for which the variation is the same as that allowed by the customer. The process is then said to have a capability index of 1. This is derived by dividing the range allowed in the specifications (2 watts) by the range of the process (2 watts). If you can reduce the variation further, you can increase the capability index to 2 or more watt specifications (range divided by 1 watt process range). Many customers want a capability index greater than 1 to insure that normal wear or some unusual process event is less likely to lead to products or services that do not meet their specifications.

? Questions to Ask

- Will it be useful to compute a capability index? To help analyze the process? To communicate with others about the process?
- Is the process stable? Can it be made stable?
- Is the process capable of meeting the specifications? If not, what can be done?
- Is the process average approximately at the center of the specification limits? Can the process target be changed to center it?

! Points to Remember

- To be capable of meeting customer specifications a process should be stable, have an aim point near the center of those specifications, and a range equal to or less than the specified range.
- With a centered aim point, an index greater than 1 indicates the process can meet specifications. The higher the index, the more room you have to meet customer specifications. An index less than 1 means the process will produce some product or service outside the specifications.
- Some people compute the index by dividing the process range by the specification range rather than vice-versa. Be sure any discussion of the index with others has the computation defined.
- If the process average is not centered within the specifications limits, an index must be computed separately for the upper and lower limits.
- You can have a capable, unstable process as well as a non-capable, stable process. Processes, can of course, be both non-capable and unstable.

Imagineering

Imagineering is visualizing how things would be if everything were perfect—no problems, no complexities, no errors, no troubles of any kind. It is the most powerful tool of all for discovering, quantifying and eliminating waste.

No one expects perfection, so asking what perfection would be like is a non-threatening way of opening people's minds to the possibilities of improvement. Imagineering is most effective when practiced with a group of people with varying perspectives on a process. It is ongoing, not a one-time brainstorming session. Although it depends on imagination, it is grounded in facts. The more a group knows about an operation, the better it will be able to imagine the "perfect" process.

Following are some of the key elements in successful imagineering:

- Imagineering can be done by individuals, but for major processes it is best done in groups. Different people offer different perspectives and ideas.

- Enlist the help of people who are involved in the process to be studied.

- Maintain an open atmosphere and give amnesty. Concentrate on perfection, explore the potential for improvement, and forget assigning blame.

- Gather facts and data to get a solid picture of current reality. Imagineering is a flight into the future, but a thorough understanding of your present position will provide far more tangible ideas about what perfection might look like. By comparing the imagineered perfection with a realistic map of the present you can discover the things needed to achieve your goals. Use flow charts, Pareto charts, benchmarking and other tools as appropriate.

- Imagineering opens people's minds to opportunities for improvement. Even people who are not naturally creative can make exciting contributions. By studying the facts and understanding customer needs and using variation, people can see why the process is not perfect. Knowing those "whys" in detail and freeing your mind from typical constraints, will make it easier to imagine what must be done to eliminate the troubles and problems.

- Imagineering fosters teamwork. As one person builds on another's ideas, people develop a shared vision to work toward.

- Imagineering is not just for use during a group session. It is a way of thinking about all processes, all situations without waste or wasted opportunities of any kind. By always comparing how things are with how they could be, people see what elements need improvement. Imagineering tells you where to work. It opens people's minds to achieving improvement on a continuous basis.

- As Henry David Thoreau said, *"People seldom hit what they do not aim at."* Imagining perfection provides a target which does not limit the opportunities for improvement.

? Questions to Ask

- What process or operation should be imagineered?
- Which people know enough about the process to contribute to an imagineering session?
- What would the process be like if everything were perfect?
- What is the difference between the current process and the imagineered process? Where are the problems, errors and complexities? Where is the waste?
- Are enough facts and data available? Have you looked outside your area, your organization or your industry for ideas to expand your thinking?
- What is needed to approach perfection?

! Points to Remember

- Use imagineering all the time.
- Ask others who are involved in the process to imagineer with you.
- Gather data and base the imagineering on facts and knowledge of the process.
- Foster an open atmosphere and encourage new and different ways to think about the process.
- Develop an action list as a result of your imagineering.
- Imagineering should be a pervasive and ongoing way of thinking.

The Affinity Process

A useful Management and Planning Tool is the Affinity Diagram. Unlike the simple charts which help us to organize <u>data</u>, this tool helps to organize <u>ideas</u>.

Use of the Affinity helps to group "like" items and then provides a theme or "header" for each group of ideas.

This process helps to:

- sort a large number of ideas quickly
- organize random thoughts into logical groupings while retaining the integrity of the original ideas
- build consensus; avoid prolonged argument
- make logic visible
- stimulate independent thought and greater variety of ideas
- make it difficult for someone to totally dominate the "discussion"

Steps to Construct an Affinity Diagram

- State the issue in general terms, typically in the form of a question.

- Brainstorm and record the ideas about the issue on cards or Post-It™ notes—1 idea per card.

- Place the Post-Its on the wall, table or flip chart—randomly.

- Sort the Post-its. Do so in silence! Look for relationships among the ideas. Work independently, moving the cards into groupings. Sometimes cards belong in more than one grouping. Make a duplicate card.

- Develop header or theme cards for each group of ideas which capture the thread of the ideas in the column. Make them clear and concise. Complete sentences that answer the question posed and include a noun-verb combination work best. Place the header card at the top of the column or grouping. Put a box around the header to distinguish it from other ideas.

- Review the affinity. Decide what you are going to do with this information.

An example of the Affinity Process is shown on the next page.

Barriers To Successfully

People are too busy	Communication is poor throughout the organization	We lack necessary resources	We lack necessary education
No time for more work	Inability to sell the program up and down the organization	Lack of funding for training and education	"Paradigm paralysis"
Lack of time to implement	Conflicting messages	No on-going coaching/ facilitation	No understanding of systems thinking
We have to reorganize first			Management belief that they don't need outside help
Too busy firefighting			

Implementing Continuous Improvement

We have a culture of fear & lack of trust	Rewards & recognition do not support new system behavior	We lack necessary skills	Leaders do not lead by example
Lack of trust	WIIFM	Illiteracy within organization	Lack of clear direction
Fear of failure	People's traditional power centers threatened	Lack of basic math skills	Management's lack of understanding of their role
Dead bodies left after down-sizing	No consequences for not participating in C.I.	No understanding of how to work effectively in teams	Lack of visibility of senior management
Fear in the organization. Unwillingness to share info	Performance appraisal system that pits people against each other	No understanding of work improvement	Lack of credibility of management
	Resistance to change	Lack of effective system of measurement to track results/progress	No visible leadership from the top
	No crisis/no reason to exert the effort		Management not knowing questions to ask to get help
			Management has no vision
			No clear direction
			No role models

Prioritization Matrix

Another Management and Planning Tool is the Prioritization Matrix. Use this tool to:

- help decide what to work on
- help to determine the relative weight of criteria for decision making
- provide a logical and visible process for decision making

Making a Simple Prioritization Matrix

- List the items to be evaluated
- Select criteria against which the items will be evaluated
- Determine the rating scale and relative weights of criteria
- Rate each item against each criterion and multiply by the weighting
- Total ratings
- Pareto the results
- Do "gut feeling" check on results
- Decide what to work on

The following is an example of a simple prioritization matrix—Choosing Suppliers for Product Line A.

The Elm Company wants to determine whom they should use as a supplier for Product Line A. They decided that the criteria are Short Lead Time, Superior Product Quality, and Low Total Cost. Further, they decided that Low Total Cost was the most important (weight = 2), Superior Product Quality was next in importance (weight = 1.25), and Short Lead Time slightly less important (weight = 1). The weight will be multiplied by the rating.

Choosing Supplier for Product Line A

Factor (Weight)

Suppliers	Lead Time 1 = > 30 days 5 = < 5 days (1)	Product Quality 1 = Adequate 5 = Outstanding (1.25)	Total Cost 1 = Highest 5 = Lowest (2)	Total
Dogwood	3	4	2	12
Maple One	2	5	4	16.25
Oaktree	4	3	3	13.75

Maple One: 2 (1) + 5 (1.25) + 4 (2) = 16.25
Oaktree: 4 (1) + 3 (1.25) + 3 (2) = 13.75
Dogwood :   3 (1) + 4 (1.25) + 2 (2) = 12

Elm decided to work with Maple One because of Low Total Cost and Superior Product Quality. Elm and Maple One agreed to work together to identify and eliminate the reasons for long lead times.

Section 2:

Work & Work Analysis

The tools of variation presented in Section 1 can help to identify and quantify waste. But to eliminate waste you also need to understand the work that is being done and how it is done. The waste comes from working on the wrong things and from not using the best process when working on the right things.

Section 2 defines the various categories of work and introduces the tools of work analysis that will enable you to plan, study, change, and improve work.

Work

We study work because all waste comes from work and work processes—what we work on and how we do the work. Most waste comes from working on the wrong things. A lesser amount comes from working inefficiently on the right things.

Work Defined - a set of tasks performed by people, machines, energy, computers, chemical processes, water, air, etc. to meet an objective, measured by the time taken, its cost and the resulting quality.

The right things to work on are those that create, deliver and add value from the external customer's viewpoint. Maximizing the time spent on value added work is a powerful tool in eliminating waste. Always ask the question "Would our customers think this activity enhances the product or service they buy from us?" Experience indicates that most organizations spend less than 25% of the time on value added work.

A typical organization spends 40% of its time on unnecessary tasks, 5-15% on necessary but not value added work, and 25% of payroll hours not working.

The Way We Work

- 10% Unnecessary Work (Other)
- 15% Necessary Work
- 25% Not Working
- 30% Unnecessary Work (Rework)
- 20% Value Added Work

This leaves only 20-30% of the time for real value added work. *That is why analyzing work is so effective in eliminating waste. By reducing or eliminating unnecessary tasks and streamlining necessary activities, it is easy to see how to make huge gains in productivity.*

Classifying Work

To start work analysis, put all the work into the categories shown in the pie chart.

Value Added Work includes such things as making a sales call, operating a lathe, preparing an invoice, making a printing plate, developing and merchandising a new product, painting a room—anything that adds value for the external customer.

Necessary Work does not add value for the external customer, but is necessary to keep the organization running. It includes such things as filing tax returns and systems maintenance. Other "necessary" tasks may not always be truly necessary. Preparing paperwork for an order may be eliminated in some cases if the process allows your customer to enter the order directly into your computer. What is necessary today may be unnecessary tomorrow. Other activities such as approval of expense reports may be done on a sampling basis or eliminated altogether.

Unnecessary Work is broken into two sub-categories: *rework and all other*. **Rework** is the most important cause of waste. This waste includes the work done incorrectly the first time, inspections to find the errors, and the work required to correct those errors.

Unnecessary Work - all other includes time spent reading or preparing reports that aren't used, performing functions that are no longer needed and in general, working on things that don't add value either to the customer or the organization.

Not Working - payroll hours spent **not working** can also be broken down into two parts—*authorized and not authorized*. Authorized time includes such things as vacation, holidays, and breaks. Time not authorized includes idle time, waiting for work, waiting for instructions, etc. Most of unauthorized not working time is driven by the system or process.

Sampling Work

While people frequently estimate how they spend their time, such estimates are usually very inaccurate, especially for people who do lots of non-repetitive work (sales people, lawyers, customer service people). Work sampling provides sufficient accuracy to be useful. It can be done with the chart shown below and a random timer. Electronic random timers, along with copies of the form shown, are available from Conway Management.

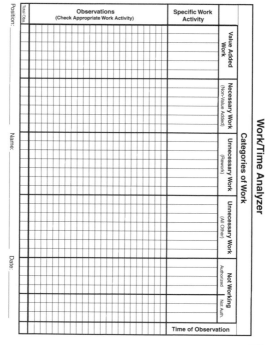

Categories of Work

To use the chart, each person should write down all of his or her activities across the top of the chart. Additional ones can be added as they arise. Participants should make the categories broad enough so that they are not adding a new activity almost every time they take a sample. Some typical activities for a salesperson would be:

- Phoning/emailing customers to promote sales
- Phoning/emailing customers to resolve complaints (rework)
- Planning sales calls
- Learning about new products
- Travel (necessary)
- Entertaining customers

Study yourself first. This will give you a feeling for the problems of classification, and it will help you understand how much time is wasted doing activities that do not add value. Involve participants early in the planning for a study. Make it clear that the purpose is to help the whole organization do more meaningful work, not to find poor performance. Let people know you will share the results of the study. Use the pie chart to indicate you expect to find a lot of waste. Share your own work sampling results to demonstrate amnesty and the need gather accurate data. Show that the purpose is not to judge any individual, but to find the 90% + of the problems that are caused by the process, the system. People will only cooperate if they perceive it to be in their interest.

A large number of observations is usually needed to get a sufficient degree of confidence in the results. As a rule of thumb, you should have at least 400 observations. Getting accurate estimates of minor activities is difficult—another reason for not dividing the activities too finely.

When the results are accumulated, make a Pareto chart of the work categories. This will give you an initial idea of how people's time is spent. Ask "Do I like what the Pareto tells me? What percentage of the time is spent on value added work or on a specific activity?" Then make a sub-Pareto chart of each category to help determine your priorities for eliminating waste.

Focus on the time spent on rework and unnecessary work. Decide on a specific activity that is taking up too large a percentage of your time. Begin a project to study the work to discover and eliminate the root causes of the unnecessary work. You may need additional work sampling studies, process analysis and other tools to understand the work more fully.

? Questions to Ask

- What is its worth to the customer?
- How does that compare to its cost?
- Is the purpose of the task still valid?
- What risks would eliminating it pose?
- Is it being done by the right person or department?
- Can it be transferred to someone outside the company?
- Can it be consolidated with some other job within the company?
- Can the frequency of the service be lowered?
- Can the content of the service be reduced?

- Can the number of people or groups receiving the service be reduced?
- How can the work process be improved?
- Can the methods be changed to make the job more efficient?
- Can the work be mechanized or computerized?
- How much time is spent waiting for work?
- Can the work load be leveled and/or can the work force be varied as needed?
- What can be done to understand the process better, eliminate causes of non-value added work, and improve the quality, cost and effectiveness of value added work?

! Points to Remember

- Much of the waste comes from working on the wrong things.
- The right things to work on are those that add value for the external customer.
- Classify the work activities into value added, necessary, unnecessary (rework or other), and not working (authorized or not authorized).
- Do a work sampling study to get a picture of what work is being done. Study yourself first.
- Focus on the improving the process, not blaming the people. 90% or more of the waste comes from the process.
- Make a Pareto chart of the types of activity. Make more detailed Pareto charts as necessary to find the waste.
- Question the need for, and value of, all the work.

Measurement

Continuous improvement depends upon identifying and tracking the right **process measures** to improve and control process variables and the right **results measures** to evaluate progress.

Measurement is one important way to "keep score". Effective measures are essential for focusing your efforts and getting (obtaining) and keeping results. Are the changes and interventions making a difference? Are they helping as much as anticipated? If so, great. If not, then you need to go back, study the process and consider other changes which will drive the measurements to the desired level.

For measurements to be useful, they must have clear operational definitions. Operational definitions are clear, concise, agreed upon descriptions of what is to be measured so that anyone collecting data will have the same understanding of what should be recorded.

Useful measures are:

- relevant
- specific
- measurable in units
- accurate
- documented
- used as part of a feedback system to monitor progress and make improvements

Determining what is important to measure before you begin your data collection efforts will provide proper focus and can save a lot of time, effort and money.

What to Measure

- **Results** - measures that reflect the overall outcome of the process or system. Results measures generally include measures of:

  Effectiveness: how well the process, product, service or system accomplishes its purpose or objective. Measures of effectiveness include customer satisfaction, quality, quantity (throughput, volume) and capability.

  Efficiency: how much it costs or how long it takes to produce the product or service. Measures of efficiency include time and cost.

- **Process** - measures that reflect parts of the process or key process variables that contribute to the overall result

- **Quality** - results measures for elements in the system or process that could be negatively impacted by improvements directed solely at overall measures. For example, if you are trying to reduce cycle time, it may be important to measure the quality and cost of the output to make sure that as cycle time is reduced, quality and cost do not suffer.

Examples of Performance Measures

Process	Quality	Quantity	Time	Cost
Production	• % on hold or rejected	• Production per hour • % yield	• Line speed • Downtime • Changeover time	• Product loss $ • $/lb packed • $/unit produced
Maintenance	• Number of repetitive failures • Mean times between failures	• Work orders completed per day	• Response time • Unscheduled downtime • Time to repair	• Cost per month • Cost per piece of equipment
Engineering Design	• Number if internal change orders • Warranty claims	• Designs per month	• Hours to design • Cycle time to do design • Backlog	• Cost of design • Life cycle cost
Order Entry	• Number and % of errors - total and by type	• Transactions per hour	• Elapsed time from customer request to delivery scheduled	• Cost of entering an order
Purchasing	• % of incoming materials out-of-specification	• Purchase orders issued per person	• Elapsed time from request to order placed • % of time spent expediting	• Cost of purchasing function as a % of total purchases • Reductions in unit cost

Keep in mind the following measurement principles:

- People pay attention to what is measured. Choosing the right measures and making them visible is critical.

- Measure to evaluate, improve and predict future process performance, not simply to judge past performance.

- Use measures as feedback to improve the process or system.

- An effective measurement system usually includes financial, customer satisfaction, business process and people capability indices.

- Measures reflect the performance of the process, not just the people.

- Consider the accuracy and reliability of your data when drawing conclusions.

- When in doubt, use 30 data points as a rule of thumb for basis of analysis.

A well-constructed measurement system can be a powerful incentive for improvement. When people are working hard to improve, they like to see the results on a regular basis. Involving the people who do the work in developing and using the measurement system creates ownership for the measures and enhances your improvement efforts.

Measure both processes and results. The world is full of people improving processes that don't affect significantly the quality or cost of a product or service.

Time & Cycle Time

Full time meaningful work that creates value for customers should always be available to each employee. Lack of such work is the biggest waste in most organizations.

Within broad limits, productivity is determined by: 1) the amount of useful work to be done, and 2) the number of people to do it. Dividing #1 by #2 gives a simple measure of productivity. Matching value added work with the workforce is not easy, but doing it well reduces a major source of wasted time.

Time Wasters

There are many system reasons why people may not have full-time value added work to do. These can include:

- Uneven work schedules.

- Establishing the work force size to meet peak loads.

- Adding a safety factor so that deadlines are always met.

- Waiting for work as part of the process.

- Bottleneck operations.

- Inadequate training or instructions.

Efforts to even the work flow and/or create a flexible workforce often can reduce waste dramatically. People want meaningful work and don't like to think their effort is wasted. But if meaningful work is not available, people may slow their pace and/or work on things that don't add value.

Another approach to reducing wasted time is to reduce the cycle time for all activities. This covers: merchandising products in a grocery store, inserting a part in an assembly, collecting receivables, preparing a budget, developing a new product, etc.

If one company can receive an order, ship the product and collect the cash much faster than another, it will have a strong competitive advantage and its costs will be less. The time it takes to develop and introduce a new product, whether it is a computer, an automobile, a box of crackers, or a toy, can make a huge difference in the sales of that product.

Built into almost every process are unnecessary delays and unnecessary steps. Examine each process in detail to see how it could be accomplished more quickly. Reducing the cycle time almost always reduces waste. It is also a key to being competitive.

Whenever you reduce the cycle time for a process, you must have a plan for how you will recapture that time and use it to do more value added work, if you expect to increase your productivity. Failure to do so often results in work expanding to fill the time available, and no measurable bottom-line improvement. You must look to either use the time to increase throughput or redeploy people or equipment to do more productive tasks.

? Questions to Ask

- Do all employees have full-time, meaningful work?
- Can the scheduling be changed to even the work flow?
- Can part-time workers and/or flexible hours be used to match the work and work force?
- Is the pace in the organization "normal?" What it should be?
- Is management setting a good example of work pace?

! Points to Remember

- The mismatch between the work force and the work to be done is a major source of waste.
- Bottleneck operations create waiting time for people and machines.
- Being faster than your competitor is a major advantage in the marketplace, and can reduce your costs substantially.

Work Simplification

Work simplification is the process of breaking work down into finer and finer pieces in order to identify and eliminate unnecessary work, unnecessary operations or motions, troubles, problems, errors and complexities.

Once you have determined that an activity or task is required... Analyze a task that takes a large amount of time. The more time involved in that work, the greater the opportunity for improvement. Also, look for repetitive work where a small improvement is multiplied many times over.

- Start with a flow chart. Once you have identified event times and waiting times, examine it more closely.

- It is easiest to improve a small element of work. Continue to break down the work into smaller and smaller elements, until it becomes obvious which parts are not needed, are causing trouble, or can be done with less effort.

- Analyze the value of every group of activities or motions and retain only those that are necessary. Improve the technology, equipment and methods.

- Recognize that work elements causing fatigue contribute to waste. Eliminate those elements or modify them to make them easier to do.

- The people doing the work should be involved in analyzing and improving the work.

Methods Analysis

Look at the work in fine detail. Question how everything is done and look for better methods.

It is easiest to improve a small element of work. Therefore, break down the work into smaller and smaller elements. Show these on a process flow chart along with the details of the job. These details include material handling, machine work, hand work and any other elements needed to describe how the work is done.

Question every detail. For each element ask: Why is it necessary? What is its purpose? Is the method used the best? Should the sequence be rearranged? Where should it be done? Who is best qualified? Also question the materials, the machines, the equipment, the technology, the tools, the layout, the product design, the workplace, safety. Ask questions about everything.

Try to imagineer the best possible method to accomplish the work. Keep in mind the needs of the customer. Eliminate unnecessary elements; change the process and/or technology; combine or rearrange elements. Simplify the work to make it easier, safer. Get other people's ideas.

Use methods analysis on new operations as well as existing ones. In fact you may come up with new ideas about a process if you imagine that an existing process is brand new and develop a method on a clean sheet with no regard to the present method.

Flow chart the new proposed method. Review it

with people knowledgeable about the work. Revise as necessary.

Test the new method in a limited area first. Consider safety, quality, time and cost. Explain the method and its purpose to the people operating the process. Apply the new method and evaluate the results. Make adjustments as needed. Remember that no process is ever perfect; more improvements are always possible.

Be sure to give credit to everyone who helped with the methods improvement.

Work Improvement Checklist

All waste comes from some form of work. Waste comes from working on the wrong thing or from the process by which the work is done. The things people work on and/or the process must be changed to make improvement. A checklist is often useful in reviewing what to do to improve work.

Steps in Work Improvement

1) Examine the mission or objectives of the group, department, division, business, etc. Is it the right business? Right objectives? Right people? In the right place? Right organization? Right project(s)? Are people working on the significant items in each project? Are people committed to continuous improvement?

2) Identify the customers, either internal or external. Look beyond the needs of the internal customer to those of the external customer.

3) Define the customers' requirements. Survey as necessary.

4) Identify the activities required to satisfy the customer.

5) Identify the suppliers. Are they the right ones to help deliver quality products and services?

6) Define requirements for suppliers. Use value analysis and value engineering as appropriate.

7) After observing the work, select a process to

improve. Work sampling will show areas of waste. Observations will detect warning signals such as bottleneck operations, wait time, schedule delays, fatigue, frustration, scrap and rework.

8) Make process flow charts. Decide what level of detail is needed. Include suppliers and customers where appropriate. Collect data. Imagineer.

9) Ask the questions of work improvement. Eliminate? Change? Combine? Rearrange? Simplify? Ask the questions in that order.
   - **Eliminate?** Look for steps that can be eliminated: movement of material, inspections, delays, filing, reporting, etc.
   - **Change?** The way the work is done? The way some steps are done? The scheduling? The technology?
   - **Combine?** Some parts of the work to improve it? With an operation in another department?
   - **Rearrange?** To make it simpler? To eliminate waste?
   - **Simplify?** Don't simplify work that should be eliminated. Simplify what is left.

10) Make the improvements. Use the Process Improvement Methodology.

11) Ensure the improvements are permanent by verifying that the people operating the process understand the improvements and are trained to carry them out. Set up a system to measure the improvement and monitor the progress. Identify further improvements.

Value Analysis & Engineering

To avoid waste, use only materials and specifications that add value to the product or service. The value analysis process examines the value added by the specified materials, usually purchased materials.

Value analysis can range from a simple discussion or brainstorming session to a formal process for examining the product's functions and determining the worth that each element contributes to those functions. The unique feature of this approach is that it concentrates on the function of the product or service and seeks to eliminate costs that don't contribute to that function(s).

How to Conduct Value Analysis

Start with a worthwhile project.

- Assemble a team with knowledge of the product or service but with different backgrounds. Include purchasing and engineering, if possible.

- Identify the functions of the product or service, always from the customer's or user's viewpoint.

- Starting with the major cost elements, analyze how each contributes value to the functions that have been identified. Can the same value be achieved at a lower cost? Can the value be improved at equal or lower cost?

- Examine your specifications. Are they too tight or too loose? Work with your supplier(s) to find out how you can lower their costs. Over-

and under-specification are major causes of waste.

- Examine alternate materials. Brainstorm. Be creative in looking for new ways to produce the same or better functional properties.

- Look at the design of the product or service. If appropriate, re-engineer it. Find a less expensive way to satisfy customer needs. Ask your customer to help you lower your costs.

❓ Questions to Ask

- What are the customer's needs/wants for the product/service?
- What functions does the customer want?
- How will the customer use the product or service?
- What does the product or service need to be able to do?
- What characteristics of the product or service allow it to perform the desired function(s)?
- What characteristics does it have that are not required?
- What can be eliminated?
- How can the functions be performed at a lower cost? How can you work with your supplier and customer to achieve a more cost-effective process?

Section 3:

Implementing Change

The first two sections have described what to do and the tools to use to achieve continuous improvement. This final section describes how to pick projects and form teams. It outlines changes to the human relations system that are necessary for people to see that it is in their interest to help. It shows how these system changes extend to suppliers and customers.

Projects

The most important decision we make is what to work on. We can't do everything that seems desirable or even urgent. Effective project selection is critical to success.

Major objectives can best be achieved through a series of projects, each focusing on a specific goal. Project ideas should all be evaluated for their potential to eliminate waste, including waste of opportunities.

Ideas can come from many sources including imagineering, and surveys of employees, customers and suppliers. Ideas can also come from identifying problems and opportunities from operating and financial reports, Pareto charts, run charts and flow charts. Anyone from the chief executive to the hourly employee has worthwhile ideas.

Most importantly, ideas should come from the process of identifying, quantifying and eliminating waste.

There are three major types of projects:
- Major management directed projects and subprojects
- Personal projects
- Other projects

Management Directed Projects
Every organization has limited resources. Management must insure that the most important and worthwhile projects have the required resources. It must also provide the direction and

follow-up for those important projects. These projects need a special designation such as "management directed projects" to make sure everyone recognizes their importance. Depending on their size, most organizations can only support 1 to 10 of these projects effectively. They include: significant quality improvements, major cost reductions, important new product developments and major changes in marketing or distribution.

The person directing the project need not be the team leader but must at least make sure that resources are made available and roadblocks eliminated. This person is often called the sponsor.

Major projects usually generate a number of sub-projects. The responsible person usually coordinates the sub-project teams to insure they are supporting the main project.

Personal Projects
Although anyone may have a personal project, it is important that each manager should do the work for at least one. This helps them to understand the process of continuous improvement and sends a message that project work is an important part of everyone's job. These personal projects should be both visible and significant.

Other Projects
Other projects should be started throughout the organization as a result of regularly identifying issues or opportunities. Small groups, departments and areas should be encouraged to start projects where they see a need, with the understanding that the resources to support their efforts may be limited. However, it is critical that these teams

have some training in gathering data and using the tools of variation, as well as the process improvement methodology and teamwork.

Control and reporting should be minimized, but managers should know what is happening in the projects in their area. They should provide encouragement, support, and appropriate direction to ensure people are working on projects that are aligned with key business goals and that improvement efforts are successful.

Project Teams

Projects are most successful when the right people are on the team. Team members should include people who do the actual work, are customers or suppliers for the process or who have a stake in the outcome. Resource specialists can also be used when the team needs their specific expertise.

Besides having knowledge of the process, people should be willing participants. Team members should help define the objective of the project and how the work is to be done. A team of 4 to 8 members usually works best. The team leader should be someone who has some ownership for the process. This person should have good leadership, communication, and analytical skills as well as meeting management skills. The leader does not have to hold a management or supervisory position, but that is often the case, especially for initial projects.

Team members should be trained to use the tools of variation—as a group, if possible. To ensure that the training is fresh in people's minds, it should come just before it is used—before the project begins and/or as needed during the project. Training in all the tools may not be necessary. The training should be adapted to the scope of the project. A facilitator who has a strong background in the tools and methods of continuous improvement can provide just-in-time training and coaching to the team. To expedite team development, include at least one team member who has had experience on another team. Availability of trainers, leaders or facilitators may limit how fast new teams are formed.

When meetings are held, prepare an agenda ahead of time to maximize the use of the team's time. Following the meeting, distribute minutes, confirming assignments and setting a time for the next meeting. The team leader keeps the project moving, obtains necessary resources, eliminates bottlenecks, works to keep the team enthusiastic and reports progress to management. The leader may change the makeup of the team if the focus changes and different people are required. The team may also bring in people with special knowledge as required. A trained facilitator is strongly recommended to improve the team's effectiveness, support the leader and provide additional training. Use the process improvement methodology as a guide for the team. When a project is finished, celebrate success, recognize everyone who helped, capture lessons learned and disband the team. For more information on teams, see *Team Waste Chasers - The Guide To Building And Sustaining High Performing Teams.*

Characteristics of Effective Teams

- Mutually set team goals
- Understanding and commitment to team goals
- Clearly defined, non-overlapping member roles
- Development is encouraged
- Decisions based on facts, not emotions or personalities
- Efficient task-oriented meetings that focus on improvement
- Discussions involve all members
- Promptly distributed minutes of team meetings
- Members listen to and show respect for each other
- Problem solving vs. blaming
- Frequent performance feedback
- Informed members
- Pride and spirit
- Free expression of feelings, ideas
- Cooperation and support of members
- Tolerance for conflict with emphasis on resolution
- Members enjoy each other

Human Relations Considerations

Good human relations help avoid the biggest waste of all—the waste of human talent. People work effectively when they perceive it is in their interest to do so. Soliciting people's ideas and showing respect for them enhances their self esteem. This is the most powerful motivator in continuous improvement. It is also the key to finding the waste.

Create a New Culture

The human relations of continuous improvement requires a whole new culture, a transformation. Changing the work system is the key to changing the culture. The "we" attitude recognizes that leaders and workers, suppliers and customers are all part of the same system, with the same goal. That goal is to run an effective organization that continually produces at low cost, quality products and services that customers want and need. Continuous improvement is required to accomplish that goal.

The team concept is critical to continuous improvement. Since all work is part of a process, the people depend on each other to produce a quality product or service. Management's role is to help and coach, rather than direct and judge. People at all levels are involved in the decision making process, which creates "ownership" for the work and for the success of the enterprise. In our experience, team members working toward continuous improvement are happy to contribute their brains and energy and feel a sense of pride in their work. Clear goals and objectives, knowledge and skills to do the work, authority to make appropriate decisions and effective feedback systems with mechanisms for reinforcement are essential for success. **Proper training is critical.** Provide the tools so that people can apply their knowledge and skills to improve the processes and systems.

Eliminate Barriers to Change

The status quo is a formidable enemy. Instead of working to preserve the status quo, as organizations often do, encourage continuous change for continuous improvement.

Here are some common barriers to change:

1. Lack of commitment by top management
2. Concerns about the ways people are judged— performance appraisal systems and merit ratings that are perceived to be unfair or that pit people against one another
3. Poor communication or poor treatment
4 Employment security concerns
5. Inadequate training
6. Lack of understanding by, and communication with unions or other key groups
7. Uncertainty about what the advantages are for the individual
8. Uncertainty about how to get started and what to do

The order of importance varies with the organization, but whenever these barriers appear, they must be recognized and systematically eliminated.

? Questions to Ask

- Are people treated as you would like to be treated if you were in their position?
- Do people recognize that 90% or more of all troubles, waste, and lost opportunities come from the process or system, not the individual?

- Do people in the organization perceive it is in their interest to share their knowledge of the best way to work, to cooperate rather than compete?
- Are there artificial caps (objectives) on the quality and productivity of the work?
- Do people know how the new system benefits them?
- Does the organization's system of rewards, advancement and recognition support people working for continuous improvement?
- Is education and training available for everyone?

! Points to Remember

- The people working in a process are the "experts" who know the process. Ask them for their help and advice.
- Continuous improvement requires teamwork. Teams mobilize the brain power and energy of the people involved in a process.
- Teams should be trained in the tools of variation on close to just-in-time basis.
- Teams require leadership by people who are dedicated to continuous improvement and who can act as coaches/players.
- Leaders enable, empower and entrust team members. They remove barriers and help generate ideas.
- Leaders are good listeners and communicators. They also observe, study and question the work and work process.
- Leaders show interest and appreciation. They handle mistakes professionally.
- Recognize, reward and promote those who work diligently for continuous improvement.

Surveys

The people with the most knowledge about the waste in a process are the operators, suppliers and customers of that process. To tap this knowledge to find the waste and opportunities, surveys can be a helpful tool.

Start by surveying the people closest to the work. They are intimately familiar with the process and know the most about the waste, problems and complexities. Prepare a list of questions that concentrate on the problems caused by the process itself. Don't get mired in problems caused by individuals or by personality differences. Test the questions by sitting down informally, one on one, with two or three people and see if the questions are effective in getting at the waste or opportunity. Also encourage a general discussion of the process.

Conduct informal surveys if a process has few people involved. For large groups, follow up the informal surveys with a written survey. Besides designing the survey questions to find out what you want, you need to:

- Explain the purpose of the survey.
- Tell participants what you plan to do as a result of the survey.
- Share the results with the people surveyed.
- Develop and carry out a plan that uses the information gathered.

These steps are important to obtain honest, open responses and to keep the respect and support of those being surveyed.

- Design surveys of internal and external customers not just to discover problems, but also to determine how you can better meet customers' needs and wants. Be prepared to respond promptly to any concerns customers express. To avoid being overloaded, and to learn by experience, start small with a few customers.

- Survey internal and external suppliers in a similar manner. Learning how to work with suppliers as a team will benefit you both. Both parties can eliminate waste by learning each other's needs and working together.

For more information about employee surveys or customer surveys, please contact us.

? Questions to Ask

- Who are the people who know the most about the process(es)?
- What do we want to determine from the survey?
- What is the best way to communicate the questions to the survey participants?
- Are resources available to respond to concerns uncovered by the survey?

! Points to Remember

The purpose of a survey should be to find the waste of material, capital, time, energy, talent, and from lost sales or opportunities.

- Make sure participants understand the purpose is to find troubles in the process and not to blame individuals.
- Communicate survey results to participants promptly.
- The overall objective of the surveys is to get suppliers, operators and customers of a process working as a team to eliminate waste, problems and complexities.

Customer & Supplier Relationships

Each person working in a process is a customer of the previous step in the process and a supplier to the next step. Our job is to work as a team to optimize the process so we can consistently deliver the highest possible value to the customer at a low total cost.

Suppliers, producers and customers are all a part of a process. The dynamics of a process can be shown as follows:

All Work Is Part Of A Process

Communicating

The traditional tools of communication are specifications, prices, acceptance sampling and complaints. In a partnership with customers and suppliers, cooperative discussions, measurements, charts and facts are used. Clear understanding of the customers' needs as well as the needs and capabilities of each party encourages change for the benefit of all. Understanding often results in modifications to requirements that can reduce waste, improve quality and/or lower costs.

Customer/Supplier Teamwork

With mutual understanding, suppliers and customers can work as a team to optimize the whole process for the benefit of all. A slight change in requirements may reduce a supplier's cost substantially. Likewise a supplier may be able to make a small change in the product that will reduce the customer's cost.

Because close cooperation is time-consuming, customers who limit the number of suppliers they use have the opportunity to maximize collaboration aimed at improving quality while reducing costs. Also, each additional supplier introduces another variable into the process. Choose suppliers who want to improve operations and have the people, capital and technology to do it. Suppliers also should have established process controls and show evidence of their process capabilities. If such suppliers are not available, work with a few to help educate them in the benefits of process control and continuous improvement.

Develop feedback mechanisms based on measurements and hold ongoing discussions of each other's needs and capabilities with the objective of optimizing the overall process for the mutual benefit of customers and suppliers.

Conway Management Company provides products and services designed to help clients make rapid, long lasting and sustainable improvements.   Our products and services include seminars and workshops, books, web-based training, surveys, coaching and consulting.

Please visit our web-site at
www.conwaymgmt.com or
call us at 1-800-359-0099
for more information.